LENE KNUDSEN
PHOTOGRAPHS BY RICHARD BOUTIN

Mug Cakes

SOFT MELTING CAKES
READY IN 5 MINUTES

hardie grant books
MELBOURNE · LONDON

Contents

Chocolate special

Tutti frutti

Mug cookies

Making your own mug cakes

The mug cake is an American invention. They are quick and easy to make and come in endless variations according to what you have in your store cupboard. A delicious experience that is different every time. Here are a few tips for making successful mug cakes.

SUPER QUICK TO PREPARE

All quantities are given in spoonfuls to make it easy to prepare the cakes without having to weigh out ingredients. Having said this, tablespoons and teaspoons vary considerably in size, so here are the equivalent weights for the measures used in the recipes in this book:

– 1 level tablespoon of plain (all-purpose) flour = 8 g (¼ oz)

– 1 level tablespoon of sugar = 11 g (½ oz)

– 1 tablespoon of liquid cream = 11 g (½ fl oz)

– 1 level teaspoon of baking powder = 3 g (0.1 oz)

– 1 thin slice of butter = 10 g (⅓ oz)

– 1 slice of butter ½ cm (¼ in) thick = 15 g (½ oz)

– 1 slice of butter 1 cm (½ in) thick = 30 g (1 oz)

Carefully beat the mixture for 1 or 2 minutes before adding any flour, otherwise you will have too many bubbles forming on the surface.

The best utensils for stirring are a fork and a mini flexible spatula.

COOKING: USING THE MICROWAVE

Mug cakes continue to cook when you take them out of the microwave. Don't worry if the surface of the cake is still a little soft when you take it out, it will dry and set in a couple of minutes.

Power settings vary from one microwave to another, so you may need to reduce or increase the cooking time to get a perfect result.

Mug cakes that contain chocolate tend to dry out more quickly!

Be careful to use only mugs that are microwave safe. Don't use vintage teacups for instance.

THERE'S NO NEED TO WAIT BEFORE YOU EAT

You can eat your mug cake straight away (well, once it's not too hot). Because mug cakes are cooked in the microwave they dry out very quickly and do not keep!

You can eat mug cookies straight from the cup with a small spoon. Mug cookies are soft rather than crunchy, and should be eaten hot or warm.

Toppings

Make your mug cake even more amazing by topping it with a layer of something delicious. When you take it out of the microwave, try spreading icing, fruit coulis, cream or sauce on top.

CHOCOLATE SAUCE

Put 5 squares of chocolate in a mug and melt in the microwave for 30 seconds (800 watts). Add 1 teaspoon of neutral oil and stir well: the mixture should be nice and smooth.

CARAMBAR® SAUCE

Carambar® is a chewy, caramel-flavoured sweet made in France which is readily available on the internet. Bend 2 Carambars® and put them in the bottom of a mug or bowl with 1 tablespoon of single cream. Cook in the microwave for around 30 seconds (800 watts), then stir carefully until the sauce is smooth and set aside.

ICING

Put 4 level tablespoons of icing sugar and 1 teaspoon of water into a small bowl. Mix well with a spoon and pour over the mug cake once cooked. To finish, decorate with ½ a teaspoon of hundreds and thousands.

WHITE CHOCOLATE SAUCE

Put 6 squares of white chocolate into a mug, add 2 tablespoons of single cream and melt in the microwave (800 watts) for about 30 seconds. Take it out and stir the sauce for an even consistency. If it is too thick, return to the microwave for a further 10 seconds. Set aside.

FRUIT COULIS

Crush 6 tablespoons of red berries in a bowl with 2 level tablespoons of icing (confectioners') sugar. Mix well, then trickle some of this fruit coulis over your mug cake.

CREAM CHEESE ICING

In a bowl, mix 75g (3 oz) fresh cream cheese with a slice of soft butter ½ cm (¼ in) thick (15 g), 2 level tablespoons of icing (confectioners') sugar and 1 level teaspoon of lemon zest. Stir until nice and smooth. Take your mug cake out of the microwave and spread a thin layer of frosting over the top.

RASPBERRY CHANTILLY

Whip 250 ml (8 fl oz) of very cold cream into Chantilly cream (whipped cream flavoured with vanilla) using an electric mixer. When the cream begins to thicken, add 4 level tablespoons of icing sugar and beat until nice and firm. Add ½ a punnet of fresh raspberries and stir them in gently with a large rubber spatula until well mixed.

vanilla mug cake

INGREDIENTS

1 slice of butter 1 cm (½ in)
   thick (30 g/1 oz)
1 egg
2 tablespoons brown sugar
1 teaspoon liquid vanilla extract
1 tablespoon single (light) cream
5 tablespoons plain (all-purpose) flour
½ teaspoon baking powder

icing & decoration

4 tablespoons icing
   (confectioners') sugar
1 teaspoon water
½ teaspoon hundreds
   and thousands

Melt the butter in a bowl in the microwave for 20 seconds (800 watts).

In a mug: beat in one by one the egg, brown sugar and vanilla extract, then the cream, flour, baking powder and melted butter.

Cook in the microwave for 1 minute 40 seconds (800 watts).

Decorate with icing (see p. 6) and hundreds and thousands.

lemon mug cake

INGREDIENTS

1 slice of butter 1 cm (½ in)
   thick (30 g/1 oz)
4 level tablespoons caster
   (superfine) sugar
2 teaspoons lemon zest
1 egg
½ teaspoon vanilla sugar
4 teaspoons single (light) cream
6 tablespoons plain (all-purpose) flour
½ teaspoon baking powder

icing & decoration

4 tablespoons icing
   (confectioners') sugar
1 teaspoon water
Yellow food colouring
1 teaspoon lemon yellow
   sugar strands (optional)

Melt the butter in a bowl in the microwave
for 20 seconds (800 watts).

In a mug: beat in one by one the sugar,
lemon zest, egg, vanilla sugar, cream, flour,
baking powder and melted butter.

Cook in the microwave for 1 minute
40 seconds (800 watts).

Decorate with yellow icing (see p. 6) and
lemon yellow sugar strands.

orange
mug cake

1 slice of butter 1 cm
 (½ in) thick (30 g/1 oz)
4 tablespoons caster
 (superfine) sugar
1 egg
½ teaspoon vanilla sugar
3 teaspoons orange juice
2 teaspoons single (light) cream
4 tablespoons plain
 (all-purpose) flour
3 tablespoon ground almonds

½ teaspoon baking powder
2 level teaspoons
 chocolate chips

icing & decoration

4 tablespoons icing
 (confectioners') sugar
1 teaspoon water
1½ teaspoons orange zest
1 strip of candied orange peel

Melt the butter in a bowl for 20 seconds (800 watts).

In a mug: beat in one by one the sugar, egg, vanilla sugar, orange juice, cream, flour, ground almonds, baking powder, melted butter and chocolate chips.

Cook in the microwave for 1 minute 50 seconds (800 watts).

Decorate with icing (see p. 6), a strip of candied orange peel and a few thin slivers of orange zest.

FOR 1 MUG – 5 MINUTES – 800 WATTS

12 – *cult*

pear mug cake
with almonds

INGREDIENTS

½ pear peeled and deseeded
1 slice of butter 1 cm (½ in)
   thick (30 g/1 oz)
1 egg
2 tablespoons caster (superfine) sugar
1 teaspoon vanilla sugar
1 tablespoon single (light) cream
6 tablespoons plain (all-purpose) flour
½ teaspoon baking powder
2 tablespoons flaked almonds

white chocolate sauce & decoration

6 squares of white chocolate
2 tablespoons single (light) cream
½ teaspoon icing (confectioners') sugar

Cook the pear in 1 tablespoon of water for 1 minute 10 seconds (800 watts) in a bowl, then drain. Melt the butter in another bowl for 20 seconds (800 watts).

In a mug: beat in one by one the egg, sugar, vanilla sugar, cream, flour, baking powder, melted butter and 1 tablespoon flaked almonds. Push in the half pear and sprinkle with the remaining flaked almonds.

Cook in the microwave for 1 minute 40 seconds (800 watts).

Top with white chocolate sauce (see p. 6) and icing sugar.

banana mug cake
with choc chips

INGREDIENTS

1 slice of butter 1 cm (½ in)
  thick (30 g/1 oz)
1 egg
4 tablespoons caster (superfine) sugar
1 teaspoon vanilla sugar
1 teaspoon single (light) cream
4 tablespoons of very ripe banana
8 tablespoons plain (all-purpose) flour
½ teaspoon baking powder
1 tablespoon chocolate chips

decoration

½ teaspoon icing (confectioners') sugar

Melt the butter in a bowl in the microwave
for 20 seconds (800 watts).

In a mug: beat in one by one the egg, sugar and
vanilla sugar, cream, ripe banana, flour, baking
powder, chocolate chips and melted butter.

Cook in the microwave for 1 minute
40 seconds (800 watts).

Decorate with icing sugar.

yoghurt
mug cake

1 slice of butter 1 cm
  (½ in) thick (30 g/1 oz)
4 tablespoons caster
  (superfine) sugar
1 egg
1 teaspoon vanilla sugar
3 teaspoons yoghurt
6 tablespoons plain
  (all-purpose) flour

½ teaspoon baking powder

coulis & decoration
2½ teaspoons icing
  (confectioners') sugar
6 tablespoons red berry fruits

Melt the butter in a bowl for 20 seconds (800 watts).

In a mug: beat in one by one the sugar, egg, vanilla sugar, yoghurt, flour, baking powder and melted butter.

Cook in the microwave for 1 minute 40 seconds (800 watts).

Decorate with icing sugar and red fruit coulis (see p. 6).

FOR 1 MUG – 5 MINUTES – 800 WATTS

18 – *cult*

marbled mug cake

INGREDIENTS

1 slice of butter 1 cm (½ in)
  thick (30 g/1 oz)
3 squares of dark chocolate
1 egg
3 tablespoons caster (superfine) sugar
½ level teaspoon vanilla sugar
1 tablespoon single (light) cream
2 tablespoons ground hazelnuts
5 tablespoons plain (all-purpose) flour
½ teaspoon baking powder

Melt the butter in a bowl in the microwave for 20 seconds (800 watts). In another bowl, melt the chocolate in the microwave for 1 minute 10 seconds (800 watts).

In a third bowl, beat in one by one the egg, sugar, vanilla sugar, cream, ground hazelnuts, flour, baking powder and melted butter.

Mix a third of the mixture together with the melted chocolate.

In a mug: spoon in by turns the flavoured and unflavoured mixtures. With a knife, draw a wave in the batter to create a marbled effect.

Cook in the microwave for 1 minute 40 seconds (800 watts).

Carambar®
mug cake

1 slice of butter 1 cm
  (½ in) thick (30 g/1 oz)
1 egg
4 tablespoons caster
  (superfine) sugar
6 tablespoons plain
  (all-purpose) flour
2 tablespoons compote

½ teaspoon baking powder
1 Carambar®

Carambar® sauce & decoration
3 Carambars®
1 tablespoon single (light) cream

Melt the butter in a bowl for 20 seconds (800 watts).

In a mug: beat in one by one the egg, sugar, flour, compote, baking powder and melted butter. Push 1 Carambar® into the middle of the mixture.

Cook in the microwave for 1 minute 40 seconds (800 watts).

Decorate with Carambar® sauce (see p. 6) and top with another Carambar® broken in half.

FOR 1 MUG – 5 MINUTES – 800 WATTS

22 – *ultimate*

marshmallow
mug cake

1 slice of butter ½ cm
  (¼ in) thick (15 g/ 1 oz)
1 egg
1½ tablespoons caster
  (superfine) sugar
1 tablespoon single
  (light) cream
3 tablespoons smooth
  peanut butter

5 tablespoons plain
  (all-purpose) flour
½ teaspoon baking powder
1 marshmallow

decoration
icing (confectioners') sugar

Melt the butter in a bowl for 20 seconds (800 watts).

In a mug: beat in one by one the egg, sugar, cream,
peanut butter, flour, baking powder and melted butter.

Add the marshmallow cut into quarters
to the top of the mixture.

Cook for in the microwave 1 minute 40 seconds (800 watts).

Decorate with icing sugar.

FOR 1 MUG – 5 MINUTES – 800 WATTS

24 – *ultimate*

mug-carrot-cake

INGREDIENTS

1 egg

4 tablespoons brown sugar

½ teaspoon vanilla sugar

2½ tablespoons sunflower oil

4 tablespoons grated organic carrots

6 tablespoons plain (all-purpose) flour

½ teaspoon baking powder

1 pinch of cinnamon or French
four-spice seasoning

cream cheese topping

70 g fresh (light) cream cheese

1 slice of butter ½ cm thick (15 g)

2 tablespoons icing
(confectioners') sugar

1 teaspoon lemon zest

In a mug: beat in one by one the egg, brown sugar, vanilla sugar, sunflower oil, grated carrots, flour, baking powder and four-spice seasoning or cinnamon.

Cook in the microwave for 1 minute 40 seconds (800 watts).

Decorate with a thin layer of cream cheese icing (see p. 6).

coconut-choc
mug cake

1 slice of butter 1 cm
  (½ in) thick (30 g/1 oz)
1 egg
2 tablespoons caster
  (superfine) sugar
½ teaspoon vanilla sugar
1 tablespoon single (light) cream
6 tablespoons plain
  (all-purpose) flour

½ teaspoon baking powder
4 tablespoons grated coconut

chocolate sauce & decoration
1 level teaspoon grated coconut
5 squares of chocolate
1 teaspoon neutral oil

Melt the butter in a bowl in the microwave
for 20 seconds (800 watts).

In a mug: beat in one by one the egg, sugar, vanilla sugar,
cream, flour, baking powder, melted butter and coconut.

Cook in the microwave for 1 minute 40 seconds (800 watts).

Decorate with chocolate sauce (see p. 6) and grated coconut.

FOR 1 MUG – 5 MINUTES – 800 WATTS

28 – *ultimate*

frangipane mug cake

INGREDIENTS

1 slice of butter 1 cm (½ in)
 thick (30 g/1 oz)
1 egg
4 tablespoons caster (superfine) sugar
½ teaspoon vanilla sugar
2 teaspoons single (light) cream
½ teaspoon French bitter
 almond extract
6 tablespoons plain (all-purpose) flour
½ teaspoon baking powder
2 tablespoons ground almonds
2 tablespoons raisins
1 tablespoon Amaretto (or other liqueur)

decoration
Custard

Melt the butter in a bowl in the microwave
for 20 seconds (800 watts).

In a mug: beat in one by one the egg, sugar, vanilla sugar,
single cream, bitter almond extract, flour, baking powder,
ground almonds, melted butter, raisins and Amaretto.

Cook in the microwave for 1 minute
50 seconds (800 watts).

Serve with custard.

nutty
mug cake

1 slice of butter 1 cm
  (½ in) thick (30 g/1 oz)
1 egg
2 tablespoons caster
  (superfine) sugar
½ teaspoon vanilla sugar
1 tablespoon single (light) cream
1 tablespoon apricot jam
5 tablespoons plain
  (all-purpose) flour

½ teaspoon baking powder
1 tablespoon hazelnuts
1 tablespoon almonds
1½ tablespoons pistachios

decoration
½ teaspoon jam (jelly)
1 tablespoon pistachios

Melt the butter in a bowl for 20 seconds (800 watts).

In a mug: beat in one by one the egg, sugar, vanilla sugar, cream, apricot jam, flour, baking powder, melted butter, chopped hazelnuts, almonds and pistachios.

Cook in the microwave for 1 minute 40 seconds (800 watts).

Spread a thin layer of jam on the outside edge and stick the remaining pistachio pieces onto it.

FOR 1 MUG – 5 MINUTES – 800 WATTS

32 – *ultimate*

financier mug cake
white chocolate melt-in-the-middle

INGREDIENTS

1 slice of butter 1 cm (½ in)
  thick (30 g/1 oz)
2 tablespoons icing
  (confectioners') sugar
3 tablespoons plain (all-purpose) flour
2 tablespoons ground almonds
1 tablespoon ground hazelnuts
¼ teaspoon baking powder
1 egg white
3 squares of white chocolate

decoration
2 hazelnuts

Melt the butter in a bowl in the microwave
for 20 seconds (800 watts).

In a mug: beat in one by one the icing sugar,
flour, ground almonds, ground hazelnuts, baking
powder, egg white and melted butter.

Add the squares of white chocolate
to the top of the mixture.

Cook in the microwave for 1 minute
30 seconds (800 watts).

Decorate with roughly chopped hazelnuts.

melt-in-the-middle
mug cake

1 slice of butter 1 cm
(½ in) thick (30 g/1 oz)
1 egg
4 tablespoons caster
(superfine) sugar
1 teaspoon vanilla sugar
2 teaspoons single (light) cream

2½ tablespoons unsweetened
cocoa powder
6 tablespoons plain
(all-purpose) flour
½ teaspoon baking powder
2 or 3 squares of milk chocolate

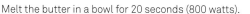

Melt the butter in a bowl for 20 seconds (800 watts).

In a mug: beat in one by one the egg, sugar, vanilla sugar, cream, cocoa, flour, baking powder and melted butter.

Push the squares of milk chocolate
into the middle of the mixture.

Cook in the microwave for 1 minute 20 seconds (800 watts).

FOR 1 MUG – 5 MINUTES – 800 WATTS

36 – *chocolate special*

chocolate fondant mug cake

INGREDIENTS

1 thin slice of butter (10 g/⅓ oz)
1 egg
4 tablespoons caster (superfine) sugar
½ teaspoon vanilla sugar
3 tablespoons unsweetened
   cocoa powder

decoration

1 square of milk chocolate
Raspberries (optional)
Small meringues (optional)

Melt the butter in a bowl in the microwave
for 10 seconds (800 watts).

In a mug: beat in one by one the egg, sugar,
vanilla sugar, melted butter and cocoa.

Cook in the microwave for 1 minute (800 watts).

Decorate with the square of milk chocolate, chopped,
a few raspberries and a small meringue.

3 chocolates
mug brownie

1 slice of butter 1 cm
  (½ in) thick (30 g/1 oz)
1 egg
4 tablespoons caster
  (superfine) sugar
6 tablespoons plain
  (all-purpose) flour
3 tablespoons unsweetened
  cocoa powder

½ teaspoon baking powder
1 tablespoon single (light) cream
2 tablespoons chocolate chips
2 tablespoons crunchy
  hazelnut spread

Melt the butter in a bowl for 20 seconds (800 watts).

In a mug: beat in one by one the egg, sugar, melted butter,
flour, cocoa, baking powder, cream and chocolate chips.

Spread the crunchy hazelnut spread
around the inside edge of the mug.

Cook in the microwave for 1 minute 20 seconds (800 watts).

FOR 1 MUG – 5 MINUTES – 800 WATTS

40 – *chocolate special*

salted caramel
mug cake

1 slice of butter 1 cm
  (½ in) thick (30 g/1 oz)
1 egg
3 tablespoons caster
  (superfine) sugar
1 tablespoon single (light) cream
2 level tablespoons
  unsweetened cocoa powder

6 tablespoons plain
  (all-purpose) flour
½ teaspoon baking powder
3 salted butter caramels
  cut into small pieces

Melt the butter in a bowl for 20 seconds (800 watts).

In a mug: add and whisk together the egg, sugar, cream, cocoa, flour, baking powder, melted butter and the chopped salted butter caramels.

Cook in the microwave for 1 minute 20 seconds (800 watts).

FOR 1 MUG – 5 MINUTES – 800 WATTS

42 – *chocolate special*

FOR 1 MUG – 5 MINUTES – 800 WATTS

Nutella® *mug cake*

INGREDIENTS

1 egg
3 tablespoons caster (superfine) sugar
4 tablespoons **Nutella®**
5 tablespoons plain (all-purpose) flour
2 tablespoons unsweetened cocoa powder
½ teaspoon baking powder

In a mug: beat in one by one the egg, sugar, **Nutella®**, flour, cocoa and baking powder.

Cook in the microwave for 50 seconds (800 watts). Leave to rest for 1 or 2 minutes before eating.

coffee-choc marble mug cake

INGREDIENTS

1 slice of butter 1 cm (½ in)
  thick (30 g/1 oz)
3 squares of dark chocolate
1 egg
2 tablespoons caster (superfine) sugar
1 teaspoon vanilla sugar
4 teaspoons single (light) cream
5 tablespoons plain (all-purpose) flour
½ teaspoon baking powder
1 teaspoon instant coffee

Melt the butter in a bowl in the microwave for 20 seconds (800 watts). Melt the dark chocolate in another bowl in the microwave for 1 minute 10 seconds (800 watts).

In a third bowl, beat in one by one the egg, sugar, vanilla sugar, cream, flour, baking powder and melted butter.

Mix the melted chocolate with the instant coffee and half of the mixture.

In a mug: spoon in by turns the flavoured and unflavoured mixtures. With a knife, draw a wave in the mixture to create a marbled effect.

Cook in the microwave for 1 minute 40 seconds (800 watts).

candied fruit mug cake

INGREDIENTS

1 slice of butter 1 cm (½ in)
   thick (30 g/1 oz)
2 tablespoons caster (superfine) sugar
1 egg
½ teaspoon bitter almond extract
1 tablespoon single (light) cream
5 tablespoons plain (all-purpose) flour
½ teaspoon baking powder
1 tablespoon candied mixed fruit, diced
2 teaspoons golden raisins
1 teaspoon blanched
   almonds cut into rounds

decoration

Custard
2 glacé cherries

Melt the butter in a bowl in the microwave
for 20 seconds (800 watts).

In a mug: whisk and add one by one the sugar, egg, bitter
almond extract, cream, flour, baking powder, melted
butter, candied fruit, golden raisins and almonds.

Cook in the microwave for 1 minute
40 seconds (800 watts).

Decorate with custard and glacé cherries .

financier mug cake
with red berries

INGREDIENTS

1 slice of butter 1 cm (½ in)
   thick (30 g/1 oz)
3 tablespoons icing
   (confectioners') sugar
3 tablespoons plain (all-purpose) flour
3 tablespoons ground almonds
¼ teaspoon baking powder
1 egg white
1 tablespoon red berries
4 raspberries

decoration

½ teaspoon icing (confectioners') sugar

Melt the butter in a bowl in the microwave for 20 seconds (800 watts).

In a mug: beat in one by one the icing sugar, flour, ground almonds, baking powder, egg white and melted butter. Add the red berries and raspberries to the top of the mixture.

Cook in the microwave for 1 minute 30 seconds (800 watts).

Decorate with icing sugar.

mug apple crumble

INGREDIENTS

½ apple peeled and diced
1 teaspoon lemon juice
1 teaspoon vanilla sugar or maple syrup
1 pinch of ground cinnamon
1 tablespoon water

crumble

1 slice of slightly salted butter
  ½ cm (¼ in) thick (15 g/½ oz)
1 tablespoon fine oat flakes
4 tablespoons plain (all-purpose) flour
2 tablespoons cane sugar
2 chopped blanched almonds

To make the crumble, mix the chilled butter, fine oat flakes, flour, cane sugar and almonds.

In a mug: mix the apple, lemon juice, vanilla sugar or maple syrup, cinnamon and water.

Cook in the microwave for 3 minutes (800 watts).

Add the crumble to the top of the mixture. Cook in the microwave for 2 minutes 30 seconds (800 watts).

tropical mug cake

INGREDIENTS

1 slice of butter 1 cm (½ in)
  thick (30 g/1 oz)
1 egg
2 tablespoons caster (superfine) sugar
1 teaspoon vanilla sugar
1 tablespoon single (light) cream
5 tablespoons plain (all-purpose) flour
2 tablespoons desiccated coconut
½ teaspoon baking powder
½ tablespoon finely chopped pineapple
1 tablespoon rum

decoration
a few pieces of fresh pineapple
½ teaspoon icing (confectioners') sugar
Vanilla ice cream

Melt the butter in a bowl in the microwave
for 20 seconds (800 watts).

In a mug: beat in one by one the egg, sugar, vanilla
sugar, cream, flour, coconut, baking powder,
melted butter, half of the pineapple and rum.

Cook in the microwave for 1 minute
40 seconds (800 watts).

Decorate with the remaining pieces of pineapple
and the icing sugar or a scoop of ice cream.

green tea mug cake
with raspberries

INGREDIENTS

1 slice of butter 1 cm (½ in)
   thick (30 g/1 oz)
1 egg
4 tablespoons caster (superfine) sugar
½ teaspoon vanilla sugar
1 tablespoon single (light) cream
5 tablespoons plain (all-purpose) flour
2 tablespoons ground almonds
¼ teaspoon matcha tea
½ teaspoon baking powder
6 raspberries

decoration
½ teaspoon icing (confectioners') sugar

Melt the butter in a bowl in the microwave for 20 seconds (800 watts).

In a mug: beat in one by one the egg, sugar, vanilla sugar, cream, flour, ground almonds, matcha tea, baking powder and melted butter.

Gently stir in the raspberries with a spoon.

Cook in the microwave for 1 minute 50 seconds (800 watts).

Decorate with icing sugar.

blueberry-ricotta mug cake

INGREDIENTS

1 slice of butter 1 cm (½ in)
 thick (30 g/1 oz)
1 egg
2 tablespoons caster (superfine) sugar
1 teaspoon vanilla sugar
1½ tablespoon ricotta
2 or 3 pinches of lemon zest
5 tablespoons plain (all-purpose) flour
½ teaspoon baking powder
2 tablespoons fresh blueberries
 (or 1 tablespoon frozen blueberries)

Melt the butter in a bowl in the microwave for 20 seconds (800 watts).

In a mug: beat in one by one the egg, sugar, vanilla sugar, ricotta, lemon zest, flour, baking powder and melted butter.

Stir in the blueberries.

Cook in the microwave for 1 minute 40 seconds (800 watts).

peanut butter mug cookie
with sesame seeds

INGREDIENTS

1 slice of slightly salted butter
  ½ cm (¼ in) thick (15 g/½ oz)
1 tablespoon caster (superfine) sugar
1 egg yolk
1 tablespoon smooth peanut butter
4 tablespoons plain (all-purpose) flour
½ teaspoon sesame seeds

In a mug: melt the butter in the microwave for 20 seconds (800 watts). Beat in one by one the sugar, egg yolk, peanut butter, flour and sesame seeds.

Cook in the microwave for 1 minute (800 watts).

mug cookie
with M&M's®

1 slice of slightly salted butter
  ½ cm (¼ in) thick (15 g/½ oz)
1 tablespoon brown sugar
1 teaspoon vanilla sugar

1 egg yolk
4 tablespoons plain
(all-purpose) flour
4 **M&M's®** roughly chopped

In a mug: melt the butter in the microwave for
20 seconds (800 watts). Beat in one by one the
brown sugar, vanilla sugar, egg yolk and flour.

Add the **M&M's®** to the top of the mixture.

Cook in the microwave for 1 minute (800 watts).

FOR 1 MUG – 5 MINUTES – 800 WATTS

62 *– mug cookie*

chocolate chip mug cookie

INGREDIENTS

1 slice of slightly salted butter
  ½ cm (¼ in) thick (15 g/½ oz)
1½ tablespoons brown sugar
½ teaspoon vanilla sugar
1 egg yolk
4 tablespoons plain (all-purpose) flour
2 teaspoons chocolate chips
1 teaspoon raisins
1 square of caramel chocolate

In a mug: melt the slightly salted butter in the microwave for 20 seconds (800 watts). Beat in one by one the brown sugar, vanilla sugar, egg yolk, flour, chocolate chips and raisins.

Add the square of caramel chocolate to the top of the mixture.

Cook in the microwave for 1 minute (800 watts).

cranberry
mug cookie

1 slice of slightly salted butter
  ½ cm (¼ in) thick (15 g/½ oz)
1½ tablespoon brown sugar
½ teaspoon vanilla sugar
1 egg yolk

4 tablespoons plain
  (all-purpose) flour
1 tablespoon dried cranberries
2 squares of white chocolate

In a mug: melt the slightly salted butter for 20 seconds
(800 watts). Beat in one by one the brown sugar,
vanilla sugar, egg yolk, flour, half of the cranberries
and 1 square of white chocolate, chopped.

Add the remaining cranberries and 1 square of white
chocolate, chopped, to the top of the mixture.

Cook in the microwave for 1 minute (800 watts).

FOR 1 MUG – 5 MINUTES – 800 WATTS

66 – *mug cookie*

gingerbread mug cookie

INGREDIENTS

1 slice of butter ½ cm
  (¼ in) thick (15 g/½ oz)
1 tablespoon brown sugar
1 teaspoon vanilla sugar
1 tablespoon honey
1 egg yolk
2½ tablespoons wholemeal flour
2 tablespoons plain (all-purpose) flour
¼ teaspoon gingerbread spices
1 sliver of candied orange peel
  (or grated zest of an unwaxed orange)

decoration

½ teaspoon icing (confectioners') sugar

In a mug: melt the butter in the microwave for 20 seconds (800 watts). Beat in one by one the brown sugar, vanilla sugar, honey, egg yolk, both kinds of flour and the spices.

Add the sliver of candied orange peel cut into tiny pieces to the top of the mixture.

Cook in the microwave for 1 minute (800 watts).

Decorate with the icing sugar.

lemon & poppy seed mug cookie

INGREDIENTS

1 slice of slightly salted butter
 ½ cm (¼ in) thick (15 g/½ oz)
1 tablespoon caster (superfine) sugar
½ teaspoon lemon zest
1 egg yolk
2 tablespoons plain (all-purpose) flour
2 tablespoons ground almonds
½ teaspoon poppy seeds

In a mug: melt the butter in the microwave for 20 seconds (800 watts). Beat in one by one the sugar, lemon zest, egg yolk, flour, ground almonds and poppy seeds.

Cook in the microwave for 1 minute (800 watts).

Acknowledgements

For Lou...
Fred, domestic mug cake martyr.
To Richard for his lovely photos and always being ready to lend a hand, thank you!
To Jennifer for her taste buds, thank you for your support, your advice and your team spirit...
To Pauline and Rosemarie for your trust, intuition and sense of proportion...
To the whole Marabout team who made this project possible!

Shopping for mugs

Iittala, www.iittala.com
Habitat, www.habitat.co.uk
Marimekko, www.marime

Mug Cakes by Lene Knudsen

© Hachette Livre (Marabout) 2013
This English language edition published in 2014 by Hardie Grant Books

Hardie Grant Books (UK)
5th & 6th Floors
52-54 Southwark Street
London SE1 1UN
T: +44 (0)20 7601 7500
www.hardiegrant.co.uk

Hardie Grant Books (Australia)
Ground Floor, Building 1
658 Church Street
Melbourne, VIC 3121
www.hardiegrant.com.au

The moral rights of Lene Knudsen to be identified as the author
of this work have been asserted by her in accordance with the
Copyright, Designs and Patents Act 1988.
Text © Lene Knudsen 2013

British Library Cataloguing-in-Publication Data. A catalogue record
for this book is available from the British Library.

With the collaboration of M&M's®.
All rights reserved.

ISBN 978-1-74270-855-3

Publisher: Kate Pollard
Senior Editor: Kajal Mistry
Translator: Gilla Evans
Typesetter: David Meikle
Photography © Richard Boutin

Printed and bound in China by 1010

10 9 8 7 6